WHAT MAKES LITTLE HONG KONG BIG TO THE WORLD?

GEOGRAPHY BOOKS FOR THIRD GRADE CHILDREN'S ASIA BOOKS

BABY PROFESSOR
EDUCATION KIDS

Speedy Publishing LLC

40 E. Main St. #1156

Newark, DE 19711

www.speedypublishing.com

Copyright 2017

In this book, we're going to talk about exploring the territory of HONG KONG. So, let's get right to it!

HONG KONG is an international city, and today it is a territory of the country of China. Because it has its own government, some people think of it as a country.

WHERE IS HONG KONG?

Hong Kong is famous for its beautiful city skyline of clustered skyscrapers and its spectacular harbor. With its blend of eastern and western influences, it is one of the most interesting places in the world and tourists from all over the globe flock there. The city of Hong Kong is situated on the southern coast of the country of China.

Macau, which is also a tourist destination known as the "Las Vegas of Asia," is 37 miles west of Hong Kong on the Pearl River Delta's opposite side.

LANTAU ISLAND

The city of Shenzhen in the Guangdong province lies north of Hong Kong. The landmass of Hong Kong is surrounded by the South China Sea. Hong Kong is made up of the Kowloon Peninsula plus over 250 islands. The largest of its islands is Lantau Island and the second in size is Hong Kong Island.

There is a waterway that separates Hong Kong Island from the Kowloon Peninsula. It is called Victoria Harbor and it is one of the deepest seaports in the world.

VICTORIA HARBOR

ABERDEEN

The words "Hong Kong" mean "fragrant harbor." On Hong Kong Island, at a place that is called Aberdeen today, sweet-smelling wood products and incense were once sold. The air in the harbor had this scent and this is how Hong Kong got its name.

WHAT ARE THE FEATURES OF HONG KONG?

The terrain of Hong Kong is hilly with steeply sloping mountains. The tallest peak is Tai Mo Shan with a height of 958 meters. There are lowlands in the northern regions.

TAI MO SHAN

PARK AVENUE, HONG KONG

More than 7 million people live in Hong Kong. It is considered very densely populated since there are about 6,700 people packed into every square kilometer of space. However, most of the people live in high-rise buildings, so the remaining space is filled with regions of greenery, such as parks and wooded areas. Because of this, Hong Kong is one of the greenest urban areas in the continent of Asia.

Hong Kong has more skyscrapers than any other city worldwide. It has more than 8,000 buildings that have more than 14 floors. That's double the number of buildings that size compared to the buildings in New York.

TYPHOON

WHAT IS THE CLIMATE IN HONG KONG?

The city is cool in the winter with heavy humidity. From the springtime through the summertime, it is quite hot and often rainy. The climate is warm with sunshine during the fall months. Hong Kong is sometimes hit with typhoons, which are enormous tropical storms.

WHAT IS THE CULTURE LIKE IN HONG KONG?

The culture in Hong Kong is a blend of Chinese traditions with western influences. The population is primarily Cantonese, from the regions of southeast China. However, there are also Shanghainese, from the Central China Coast, as well as Indian, Jewish, and British people living in Hong Kong.

CHINESE NEW YEAR PARADE

The Cantonese culture is a major influence and the traditional values of "family glory, modesty, and saving face" are common here. On the other hand, many Hong Kong citizens have adopted a way of life that is more like Western culture.

Hong Kong has a "biliterate" culture, which means that both Chinese and English are the official languages. However, much of the population is "trilingual" and the languages of Chinese Mandarin, English, and Cantonese are spoken.

The food in Hong Kong is blended too. There are flavors of traditional Chinese cuisine mixed together with western dishes. Many different foods are offered at traditional Chinese holidays throughout the year, such as the Chinese New Year and the Ching Ming Festival.

BUDDHA

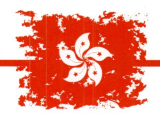

Christian holidays, such as Christmas Day, are celebrated as well although only 10% of the population is Christian. The primary religions practiced are Taoism, Buddhism, and Confucianism.

One of the art forms that Hong Kong is known for is its Cantonese opera. This performance art blends Chinese stories with drama and music to create exciting shows both in Chinese and English.

TAI CHI

Both Kung Fu, a form of martial arts that resembles karate, and Tai Chi, also known as shadow boxing, are used for entertainment as well as exercise.

In addition to being a major port in Asia, Hong Kong is an important financial center. It's the third most important financial hub worldwide after New York and London. It's also known as a destination for tourists who love to shop.

WHAT IS THE HISTORY OF HONG KONG?

The first people settled in the area that is now Hong Kong over 30,000 years ago. China incorporated the landmass into its country during the reign of the Qin Dynasty from 221 to 206 BC.

In the year 1513 AD, Jorge Alvares, an explorer sailing for Portugal set foot in Hong Kong.

JORGE ALVARES

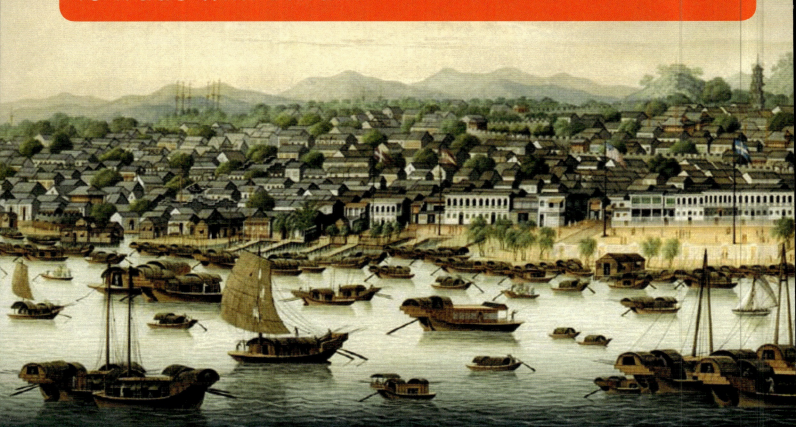

Trade was established between Portugal and China and the countries were friendly for a while. Eventually, the people of both countries began to battle with each other and trading ceased. Many years later, in the late 1600s, the East Indian Company, which was a British company, came to the port and China's Hong Kong began to trade with Britain.

TRADING

Through the centuries, Hong Kong remained mostly ruled by China until 1841. At that time, the Chinese Qing Dynasty lost the First Opium War, and the Chinese were forced to give Hong Kong Island to the British. Hong Kong became a British colony. The city grew to a major port and traded with southern China. When the Chinese government became communist in 1949, many people in China escaped to Hong Kong to retain their freedoms.

The British had ruled Hong Kong for over 150 years when it went back to Chinese rule in 1997. Today it is a "special administrative region" of the People's Republic of China, which simply means it is allowed to be independent. It's operated under a ruling called "one country, two systems."

WHAT PLACES ARE GOOD FOR EXPLORING IN HONG KONG?

There are so many places to go in Hong Kong. Here are a few exciting places you might like to visit.

STAR FERRY

Would you like to take a boat ride in Victoria Harbor? Then, you would love a ride on the Star Ferry, which has been famous in Hong Kong since 1880. It only costs a few dollars in Hong Kong money to ride, and the harbor is buzzing with activity. Ships of all shapes and sizes are sailing there as the masterful captains avoid colliding into each other.

The cluster of skyscrapers against the backdrop of beautiful green mountains provides a spectacular view from the ferry. If you travel on the ferry at night, you can see an amazing laser light show with a 360-degree view of lights that bounce off the buildings to accompanying thematic music.

VICTORIA CENTRAL BUSINESS DISTRICT

Do you love gazing at skyscrapers? Then, you would enjoy walking around the part of the coastline known as the Victoria Central Business District. There are skyscrapers everywhere you look, including the angular Bank of China skyscraper, which was once the tallest building in the city.

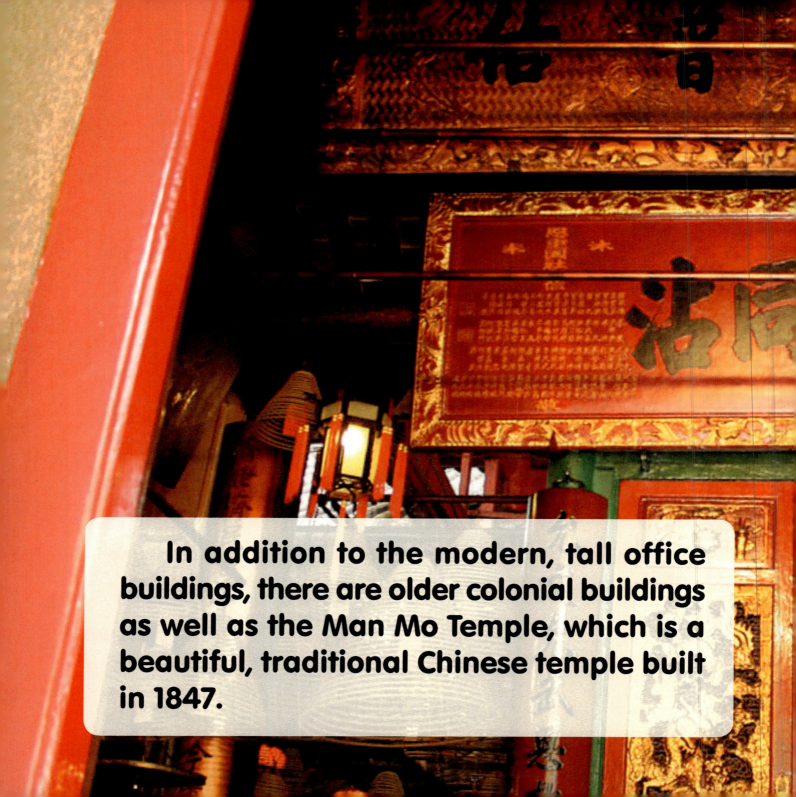

In addition to the modern, tall office buildings, there are older colonial buildings as well as the Man Mo Temple, which is a beautiful, traditional Chinese temple built in 1847.

THE AVENUE OF STARS

Would you like to see a place than honors Hong Kong's celebrities? Then, you would like to visit the Avenue of Stars. It is Hong Kong's version of the Walk of Fame that appears in California's Hollywood. One of the stars honored there is famous martial arts performer Bruce Lee. The Avenue of Stars is part of a long promenade along the waterfront in Tsim Sha Tsui where it is fun to walk, jog, and people watch as you look at the harbor vistas.

OCEAN PARK

Would you like to see a Giant Panda up close and personal? Then, you would enjoy visiting Ocean Park. You could spend the entire day there as you tour old sections of Hong Kong, ride on the roller coasters, and visit the Grand Aquarium, which is the largest dome aquarium on Earth. There are 400 different species of fish housed there as well as a Reef Tunnel adventure. After your underwater fun, you can go see the Giant Panda attraction where there are both types of Chinese pandas as well as the giant Chinese salamander, which is the largest amphibian in the world.

GLORIOUS HONG KONG!

A former British colony, Hong Kong is now once again under Chinese rule. However, it has been allowed to keep its former government under a "one country, two systems" ruling. Hong Kong is a global port, international financial center, and worldwide shopping destination. It is famous for its city skyline. It's densely populated, but, because of its skyscrapers, most people live in apartments off the ground leaving large wooded and green areas throughout the city. There are many exciting places to see in Hong Kong!

Awesome! Now that you've gone exploring in Hong Kong, you may want to visit the country of China in the Baby Professor book No, Not Chinatown! The Real China! Explorer Kids Geography Book.